Jesu, Joy of Man's Desiring

by Johann Sebastian Bach

arranged for harp solo, harp duet,

& harp, flute & voice

by Sylvia Woods

Artwork by Heidi Spiegel

This book is dedicated with love and thanks to Jeannette Debonne.

**Please contact your local harp music retailer or visit
www.harpcenter.com
for more harp music books by Sylvia Woods.**

©1992 by Sylvia Woods, Woods Music & Books
2nd Edition © 2016 by Sylvia Woods

ISBN 0-936661-12-7

Jesu, Joy of Man's Desiring, the *Chorale* from *Cantata #147*, is one of Bach's best-loved works. Sylvia Woods has created several arrangements of this beautiful music:

#1. A harp solo version for lever harp, which is an abridged version of the pedal harp solo.
#2. A harp solo version for pedal harp.
#3. An arrangement for harp duet for 2 lever or pedal harps.
#4. An arrangement for harp and flute (or violin, or other solo instrument).
#5. The harp and flute arrangement also has an optional vocal part which can be sung, or played by another solo instrument. (Note: this arrangement cannot be used with just harp and voice, it needs the flute part to be complete.)

For each ensemble arrangement Sylvia provides a "score" (with all of the instrument parts together on the same page), and also each instrument "part" on a separate page.

Table of Contents

Pedal Harpists: Pedal changes are written below the bass staff.

All Lever Harpists: Be sure to set your sharping levers for the key signature before you begin, following any additional instructions written at the beginning of each piece. All sharping lever changes are indicated in the music using both diamond notes and octave wording between the treble and bass staves. The chart below shows the octaves indicated by the lever changes in this book. "Low" indicates the octave below middle C, "mid" indicates the octave from middle C up to B, and "high" indicates the next higher octave. "Very high C" is 2 octaves above middle C.

Lever Harpists Tuned to 3 Flats: The duet arrangements require A-sharps. If you have your A strings tuned to A-flat, you will need to re-tune the two A strings shown below to A-natural before you begin. You can then use your levers to make the necessary A-sharps in the music.

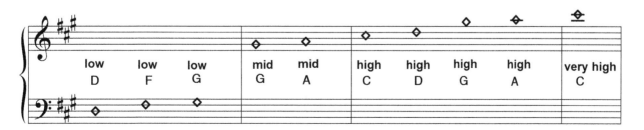

Jesu, Joy of Man's Desiring
for Solo Lever Harp

Johann Sebastian Bach
Arrangement by Sylvia Woods

This arrangement for solo lever harp is an abridged version of the pedal harp arrangement on page 6.

See page 3 for information about sharping lever changes.

Lever Harp

Jesu, Joy of Man's Desiring
for Solo Pedal Harp

Johann Sebastian Bach
Arrangement by Sylvia Woods

This arrangement is for pedal harps. Pedal changes are written below the bass staff.

Pedal Harp

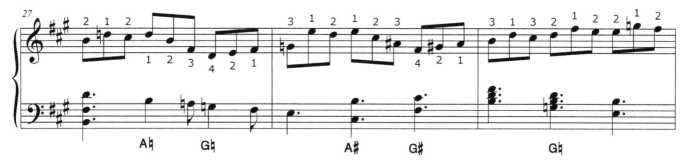

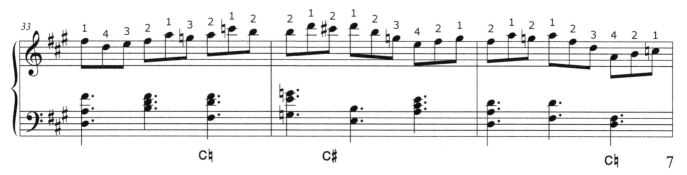

7

Jesu, Joy of Man's Desiring
Score for Harp Duet

Johann Sebastian Bach
Arrangement by Sylvia Woods

Throughout most of this duet, the melody is played by both hands in the "Harp 1" part. In certain sections, the melody is played only by the right hand, allowing the left hand to change the sharping levers on lever harps. Pedal harpists may continue the melody in octaves throughout these sections if they prefer.

See page 3 for information about sharping lever and pedal changes.

The "Harp 1" part is printed on page 15, and "Harp 2" begins on page 18.

The "Harp 2" part is the same as the "Harp Part" in the Harp, Flute & Voice arrangement on page 21.

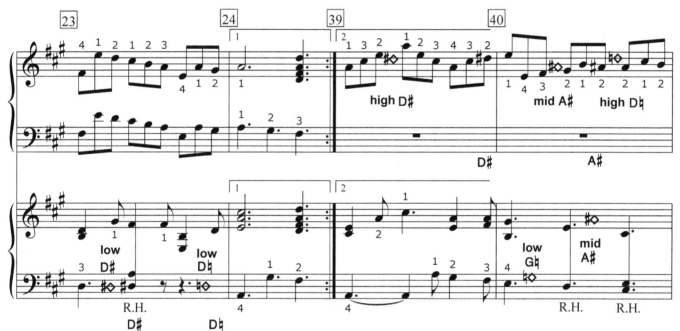

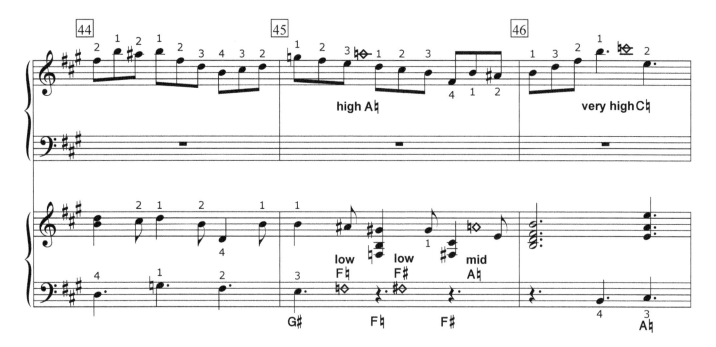

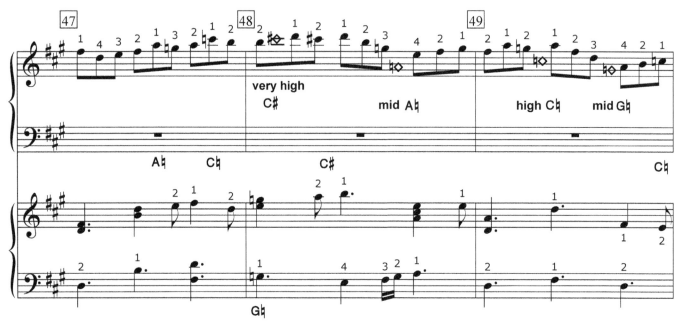

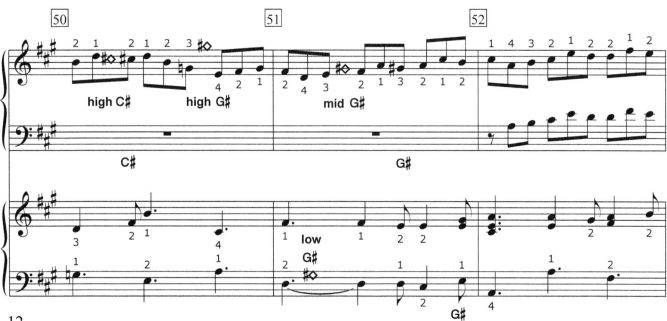

12

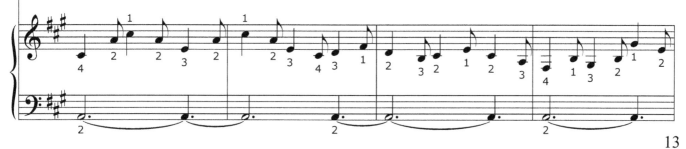

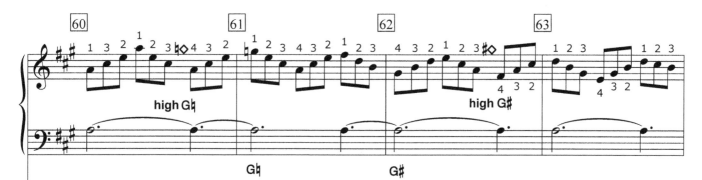

13

14

Jesu, Joy of Man's Desiring
"Harp 1" of Harp Duet

Johann Sebastian Bach
Arrangement by Sylvia Woods

Throughout most of this duet, the melody is played by both hands in the "Harp 1" part. In certain sections, the melody is played only by the right hand, allowing the left hand to change the sharping levers on lever harps. Pedal harpists may continue the melody in octaves throughout these sections if they prefer.

See page 3 for information about sharping lever and pedal changes.

The Score for the Duet begins on page 9.

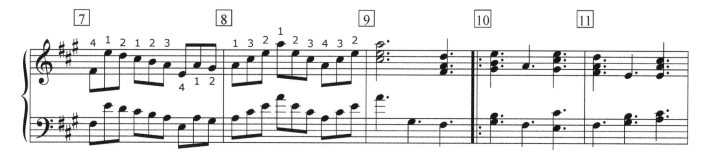

15

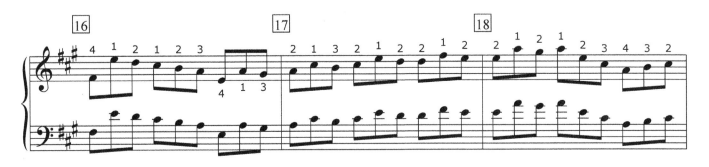

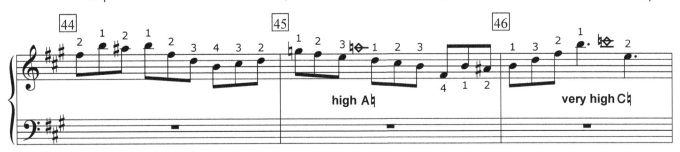

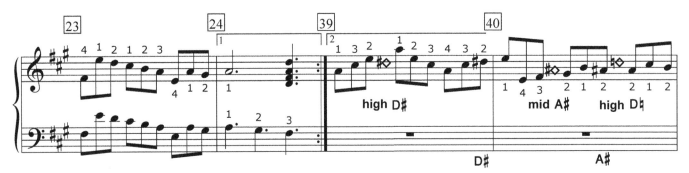

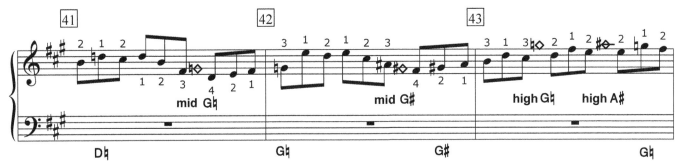

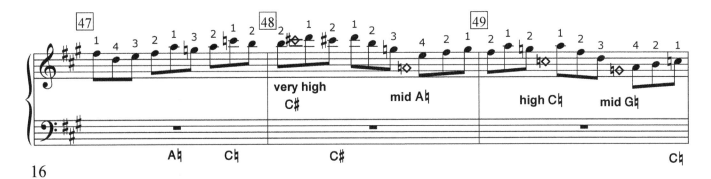

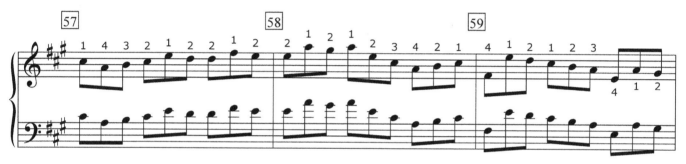

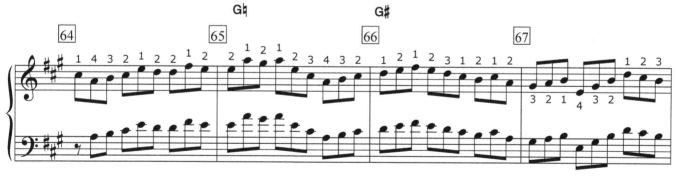

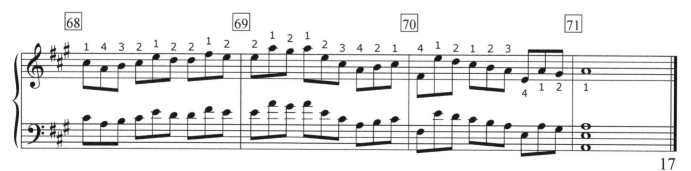

17

Jesu, Joy of Man's Desiring
"Harp 2" of Harp Duet
and "Harp Part" for Harp, Flute & Voice Arrangement

Johann Sebastian Bach
Arrangement by Sylvia Woods

This harp part is "Harp 2" of the Duet and also the "Harp Part" in the Harp, Flute & Voice arrangement.

See page 3 for information about sharping lever and pedal changes.

The Score for the Duet begins on page 9. The Score for the Harp, Flute & Voice arrangement is on page 21.

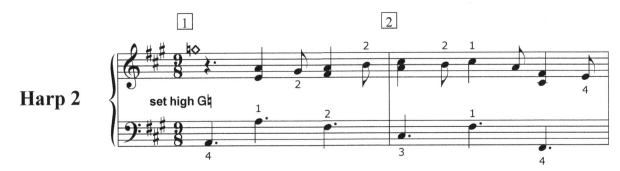

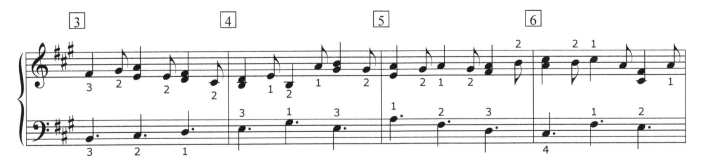

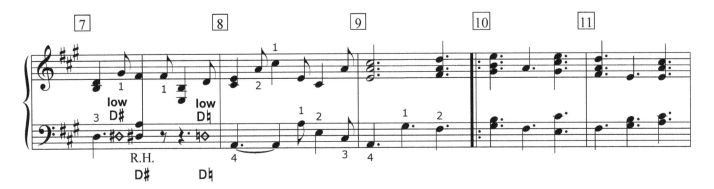

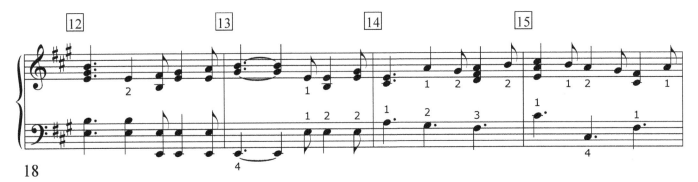

18

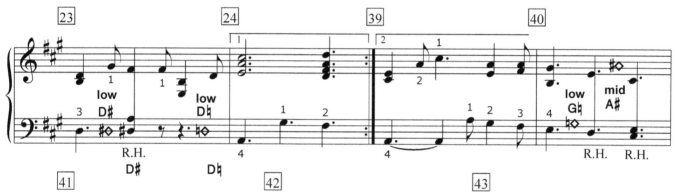

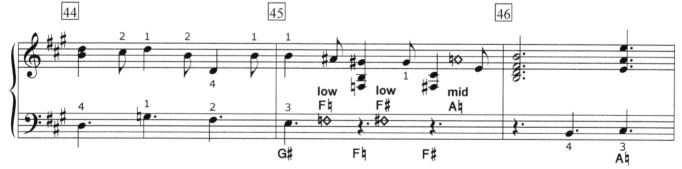

19

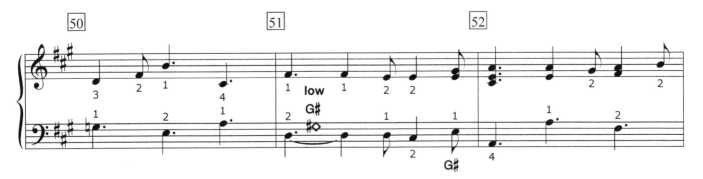

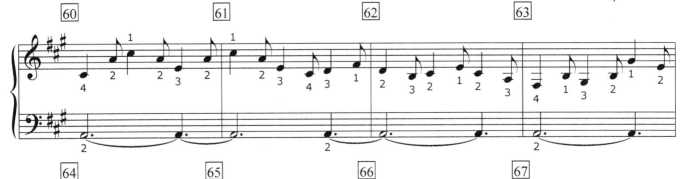

Jesu, Joy of Man's Desiring
Score for Harp & Flute (or Violin)
with optional Voice Part

Johann Sebastian Bach
Arrangement by Sylvia Woods

This arrangement cannot be used with just harp and voice, it needs the flute part to be complete.
The "Flute" part may be played by flute, violin, or other solo instrument. It is printed on pages 28-29.
It may be copied for the instrumentalist.

The "Voice" part of this arrangement is optional. It may also be played by an instrument instead of a singer.
It is printed on page 31, and may be copied for the vocalist or instrumentalist.

The harp part is the same as the "Harp 2" Duet part, and begins on page 18.

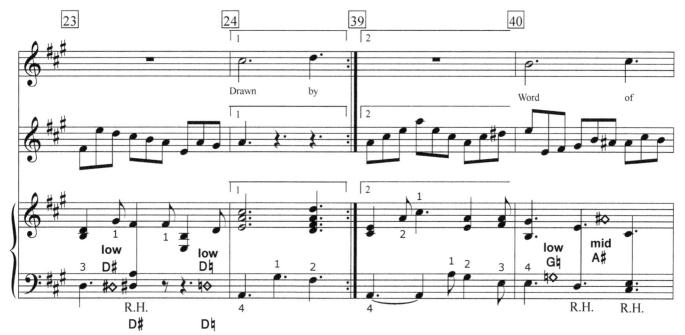

23

24

still to Truth un - known.

Soar - ing, dy - ing round Thy

throne.

26

Jesu, Joy of Man's Desiring
"Flute Part"
for Harp, Flute & Voice Arrangement

Johann Sebastian Bach
Arrangement by Sylvia Woods

This "Flute" part may be played by flute, violin, or other solo instrument.
This page may be copied for the instrumentalist.

The Score for this arrangement begins on page 21.

Jesu, Joy of Man's Desiring
"Voice Part"
for Harp, Flute & Voice Arrangement

Johann Sebastian Bach
Arrangement by Sylvia Woods

The "Voice" part of this arrangement is optional. It may also be played by an instrumentalist instead of a singer. This page may be copied for the vocalist.

The Score for this arrangement begins on page 21.